CW01512880

Original title:
Dappled Vines Along the Dragon Heap

Author: Olivia Oja
ISBN HARDBACK: 978-1-80563-428-7
ISBN PAPERBACK: 978-1-80564-949-6

Fables Carved in Ancient Bark

In the heart of the woods, secrets lie,
Carved in the bark, where old fables sigh.
Whispers of times when the magic was near,
Echoes of legends that the trees hold dear.

Moss-covered memories cling to each bend,
Tales of brave knights and the creatures they blend.
Under the shadow of branches so wide,
Stories of courage rise with the tide.

The owls hoot softly, their wisdom bestowed,
Holding the truths of the paths we have strode.
Every knot in the wood tells a tale well spun,
Of battles and truce as the ages have run.

With each gentle breeze, the boughs softly sway,
Carving out futures from the past's rich clay.
In the twilight's glow, let imagination spark,
Embrace the fables carved in ancient bark.

Twilight's Kiss on Forest Paths

In the forest where shadows dance and weave,
Twilight's kiss beckons, encouraging to believe.
Where fireflies twinkle like stars in the gloom,
And secrets are whispered in the soft night's bloom.

The trees stand tall like guardians of night,
Their branches reach out, embracing the fright.
Misty trails guide where dreams intersect,
In each step we take, hidden worlds we detect.

A chorus of crickets serenades the dusk,
Where nature breathes deeply in lessons of trust.
Softly the night wraps the forest in grace,
With each fleeting moment, eternity's face.

So wander the paths where the twilight does blend,
Feel the magic, let your weary heart mend.
In every shadow, a story unfolds,
As twilight kisses the forest's dark holds.

Harmony Found in Wild Convolutions

Amidst tangled roots, wild beauty does grow,
Nature's own canvas, vibrant in show.
In chaotic embrace, the creatures entwine,
Life dancing freely, in rhythm divine.

Petals unfold like a painter's own dream,
Colors ablaze in a sunlit stream.
In the wild convolutions, a balance is found,
Where chaos and order in harmony sound.

The river runs swift through the thickets and bends,
Carving the landscape, where neither it ends.
Each turn of the current a story of life,
In the whirl and the rush, both the joy and the strife.

Listen closely now, to the whispers of trees,
In their rooted wisdom lies a gentle peace.
For within every twist, every turn that we see,
Is the wild truth of nature's own decree.

The Symbiosis of Stone and Vine

In a dance of devotion, the stone meets the vine,
Lifetimes entwined where the sun's rays combine.
Granite and greenery, a partnership strong,
In silence they flourish, where both belong.

The vine wraps its arms around rugged old stone,
Cradling history in whispers well-known.
With each gentle twist, a bond forged in trust,
Nature's sweet love is unyielding and just.

Cast shadows and sunbeams weave stories long told,
As life takes its course, both daring and bold.
Each drop of the rain nourishes dreams that align,
Creating a tapestry, the symbiosis divine.

From roots deep below to the heights of the trees,
They flourish together, in harmony's breeze.
In the stillness of moments, let us pause and reflect,
On the union of stone and the vine's soft caress.

Whispers of Leafy Shadows

In the glen where secrets dwell,
The leaves converse in softest spell.
Each rustle tells of tales untold,
Of ancient dreams and fortunes bold.

Beneath the arch of emerald light,
The shadows dance, a wondrous sight.
With playful whispers on the breeze,
They weave their magic through the trees.

A chorus sings of ages past,
Of fleeting moments, shadows cast.
In twilight's glow, the forest sighs,
Where every leaf holds a disguise.

In secret nooks, fair creatures peek,
Weaving tales with voices meek.
Their laughter rings, a gentle chime,
As nature weaves the thread of time.

So wander deep with open heart,
Where leafy shadows play their part.
Embrace the whispers, soft and low,
In this enchanted world below.

Tangles of Green and Gold

In a world where colors blend,
The green and gold twist and bend.
Vines entwine and softly weave,
A tapestry that we believe.

Amidst the ferns, a secret glade,
Where sunlight hues begin to fade.
The golden rays that pierce the boughs,
Whisper stories, share their vows.

As time slips by on gentle streams,
The forest cradles all our dreams.
Each tangled path, a journey new,
With hidden wonders to pursue.

The rustling leaves, a harmony,
Invite the heart to dance, roam free.
In nature's arms, we lose our fears,
Embracing whispers through the years.

So venture forth, let spirits soar,
In tangled realms of evermore.
Where green and gold forever gleam,
And life unfolds a magic dream.

Secrets in the Twisting Boughs

In boughs that twist and turn with grace,
Where secrets linger, time can trace.
The air is thick with whispered lore,
Of ancient woodlands rich and core.

Each branch a keeper of the past,
The wisdom held in shadows cast.
With every creak, a tale's invoked,
Through sylvan realms where dreams are cloaked.

The moonlight spills like silver dew,
Illuminating paths once few.
In every nook and cranny found,
The spirit of the woods unbound.

Beneath the canopy so vast,
The echoes of the wild are cast.
They speak of wanderers long gone,
Who sailed through night till the dawn.

So listen well to nature's call,
In twisting boughs, come one, come all.
For in their secrets, truth reveals,
The magic that the forest heals.

The Enchanted Wreath of Nature

In petals soft, the world awaits,
A wreath of nature captivates.
With colors bright and fragrances sweet,
Each bloom a wonder, pure and neat.

The branches arch in graceful arcs,
In canopies where sunlight sparks.
Amid the blooms, the fairies play,
In every leaf, each budding ray.

With gentle hands, the earth bestows,
A crown adorned with nature's prose.
Each flower soft, each vine that curls,
A testament of magic swirls.

As seasons change, the wreath grows bold,
In vibrant splendor, stories told.
From winter's frost to summer's light,
The cycle spins, both day and night.

So wander through this verdant dome,
Let petals guide you safely home.
In the enchanted wreath of grace,
Nature reveals her warm embrace.

Climbing Hearts in a Sunlit Glade

In the glade where sunlight beams,
Hearts entwined in gentle dreams.
Whispers dance on breezy air,
Love's sweet secrets everywhere.

Soft petals blush beneath the gaze,
Of secret wishes set ablaze.
With every laugh, the shadows play,
In a symphony of bright array.

The trees sway slow, a wooden song,
In this place where we belong.
Hand in hand, we staircase high,
Underneath the sprawling sky.

Golden rays and laughter blend,
In this glade where worlds transcend.
With every step, our spirits rise,
As hope ignites and never dies.

Let the sun be our guide today,
Through the heart's enchanting way,
In the glade so warm and free,
We find love's sweet mystery.

Enigma of the Verdant Spiral

Winding paths of green delight,
Veils of mist within the night.
Each turn shows a hidden truth,
In the spiral, we rediscover youth.

Whispers echo through the leaves,
Nature's lore, a tale that weaves.
Step by step, the mystery calls,
As the verdant kingdom sprawls.

Feathered friends above us soar,
Guardians of the forest floor.
With every rustle, wisdom's gain,
In the spiral, we break the chain.

Light dappled through the emerald fray,
Guides us through the murky gray.
In our hearts, a spark ignites,
As we delve into the nights.

The enigma of this verdant maze,
Unraveling in magical ways.
Through twisting trails, we grasp the light,
In nature's arms, our spirits take flight.

Serpent's Embrace of Flora

In the thicket where shadows sway,
Nature's serpent winds at play.
A dance of vines, a quiet sound,
In the lushness, mysteries found.

Beneath the canopy so deep,
The secrets of the forest keep.
With every curl, the stories spin,
Inider tales of loss and win.

Every leaf, a whisper shared,
Of battles fought and hearts repaired.
In molten green, the magic breathes,
In the embrace of tangled wreaths.

Though shadows linger, light breaks through,
Revealing paths of emerald hue.
As serpents twist and shadows glide,
We find the magic deep inside.

With every pulse, the forest sways,
In the serpent's clasp, we gaze.
Woven in this wild embrace,
We lose ourselves, find our place.

Luminescent Trails Through the Forest

Glistening paths of silver light,
Guide us through the velvet night.
Each step illuminates the way,
As dreamers wander, born to stray.

Mushrooms glow with gentle grace,
The forest smiles in this embrace.
In shadows deep, the colors bloom,
A tapestry that sweeps the gloom.

Moonlit glades sing to the heart,
A symphony that won't depart.
Echoes of the night extend,
As magic whispers, time to mend.

Stars alight, a twinkling guide,
In this realm, our fears collide.
With every moment, hope prevails,
On luminescent winding trails.

Through the woods, the magic flows,
In the night, the wonder grows.
Together, hand in hand we roam,
In this forest, we find home.

Ember Glow in the Foliage's Veil

In twilight's hush, the leaves do glow,
A dance of fire, a softening show.
Shadows weave through branches tall,
Whispers of magic in twilight's call.

Beneath the boughs where secrets dwell,
Ancient tales begin to swell.
Embers flicker, a tapestry bright,
Nature's canvas, a wondrous sight.

Moonlight spills on velvet ground,
In every rustle, a story found.
Crickets sing as twilight lingers,
Enchanting night with silver fingers.

A spark of life in every leaf,
A moment's peace amid the grief.
Here, in the forest's embrace so tight,
The ember glow ignites the night.

Within this realm, the heart takes flight,
Carried away on dreams of light.
Embers fade, yet memories stay,
Woven in dreams, forever they'll play.

The Bounty of the Wayward Thorns

In gardens wild, where shadows creep,
   Wayward thorns in silence seep.
   Beauty masked behind the pain,
   A treasure found in loss's reign.

   Beneath the thicket, secrets hide,
   Riches buried, untamed pride.
For every thorn that pricks the skin,
   A blossom waits, a chance to win.

A sunlit path through tangled vines,
Life's gentle rhythm, sweetly entwined.
   In each sharp edge, a story sings,
Of growth and grief, and what it brings.

   With every battle, wisdom grows,
From hidden depths, the courage flows.
   The bounty waits for hearts so bold,
   To roam the wild, let wonders unfold.

So fear not thorns, embrace the strife,
   For in their grasp, we find our life.
The bounty shines in shades unknown,
In wayward thorns, true beauty's grown.

Nature's Legacy in Coiled Growth

In the heart of the forest deep,
Nature's whispers begin to creep.
Coiled growth wraps the earth in grace,
Embracing all in a lush embrace.

Each winding twist holds stories old,
Of ancient times and dreams retold.
A symphony of life unfolds,
In every curl, a secret holds.

Roots intertwine like lovers' hands,
Binding earth, creating lands.
From tangled stems, new life will spring,
A cycle spun on fortune's wing.

Every branch a legacy we see,
History bound in roots of tree.
In coiled growth, we find our place,
A tribute to time, a warm embrace.

So pause a moment, breathe it in,
The wisdom found in where we've been.
Nature's legacy quietly grows,
In coiled whispers, the heart bestows.

Visions Stitched in Greenery's Embrace

In the realm where green dreams soar,
Visions stitched through nature's core.
A tapestry of leaf and vine,
Crafting stories, softly entwined.

In every petal, a dream we share,
Whispers of hope springing from air.
Through emerald halls, we wander free,
Chasing the hues of what could be.

Sunlight dances on dewy frames,
In wild gardens where silence claims.
A sanctuary for heart and soul,
In greenery's embrace, we are whole.

With every rustle, the promise rings,
Life's gentle pulse in the songs it sings.
Weaving visions in nature's quilt,
A sacred bond where love is built.

So let us wander, hand in hand,
Through verdant paths, a magic land.
Here in the lush, our spirits trace,
Visions stitched in greenery's embrace.

The Alchemy of Leaf and Stone

In shadows deep where secrets hide,
The whispers of the forest glide,
With stone and leaf in gentle dance,
They shape the world with just a glance.

Through ancient boughs the moonlight streams,
Where time unfolds and starlight beams,
Each grain of dust a tale to tell,
Of magic wrought by nature's spell.

The roots entwine beneath the ground,
In silence weave and dance around,
And from the heart of earth they rise,
A tapestry of whispered sighs.

The branches bend, their stories sway,
In alchemy of night and day,
From leaf to stone, the cycle spins,
As echoes fade, new life begins.

In twilight's arms, the forest breathes,
A symphony that softly weaves,
So join the dance, the timeless flow,
In alchemy where wonders grow.

Garden of Whispers and Echoes

In twilight's blush, the garden sighs,
With petals soft beneath the skies,
Each flower bows with secrets old,
In colors bright and whispers bold.

The willow weeps beside the brook,
Its branches dance like a storybook,
While shadows play on cobbled stone,
In echoes of a past well-known.

Each breeze that stirs, a voice divine,
It murmurs softly, "You are mine,"
As crickets chirp their evening song,
In harmony where hearts belong.

The moonlight spills on petals fair,
Illuminates the fragrant air,
Where nightingale and dreamers meet,
In serenades so soft, so sweet.

Amidst the blooms, the magic gleams,
In dances spun from ancient dreams,
This garden holds the world's embrace,
A haven found, a sacred space.

Mirth Beneath the Sylvan Canopy

Beneath the boughs where laughter grows,
The sunlight dances, and brightly glows,
Where creatures small with joy abound,
In harmony, their hearts resound.

The playful breeze, a gentle tease,
It carries notes of rustling leaves,
And in the glade, the wildflowers,
Compose a symphony for hours.

With every step, the earth invites,
A tapestry of colors bright,
Where fairy folk and sprites convene,
In mischief sweet and sights unseen.

The canopy, a vault of green,
Where dreams are spun and hopes convene,
In every nook, a tale concealed,
In whispers soft, the heart is healed.

So linger here, in nature's cheer,
Embrace the joy, dispel your fear,
In sylvan realms, let laughter flow,
For in this place, our spirits grow.

Reverberations in the Hanging Gardens

In gardens high where silence sings,
The echoes dance on golden wings,
With blossoms spilling soft and bright,
They weave a dream in morning light.

The vibrant hues of every flower,
Unfolding peace at every hour,
While petals whisper tales of yore,
In fragrant notes from nature's core.

Each vine, a thread of history spun,
In shadows cast by setting sun,
The laughter ripples through the air,
In harmony, all hearts laid bare.

The water's edge, a mirror bright,
Reflects the magic of the night,
Where lanterns glow like stars above,
In silhouettes of peace and love.

So stroll these paths with gentle grace,
And find your heart's most sacred place,
In every step, let wonders blend,
In hanging gardens without end.

Echoes of Serenity in Leafy Lattices

In whispers soft, the leaves do sway,
Beneath the sun's warm, golden ray.
The branches cradle dreams so bright,
While nature hums a lullaby of light.

A gentle breeze, a tender touch,
In emerald halls where time moves slow.
The chatter of the sparrows sings,
A serenade of joy that grows.

Through dappled glades where shadows dance,
The spirit wanders in a trance.
With every step on mossy beds,
The heart unfurls where calmness spreads.

And when the twilight starts to blend,
With twilight hues, new dreams ascend.
In leafy lattices, peace is found,
In nature's cradle, love abounds.

So pause and breathe this pure delight,
Where echoes linger, taking flight.
In every rustle, every sigh,
The calm of nature draws us nigh.

The Celestial Weave Amidst the Wilderness

A tapestry of stars unfolds,
Above the wild, their stories told.
In silver threads of moonlit beams,
The night ignites with timeless dreams.

Among the trees, the shadows play,
Parting dusk from the break of day.
Each rustling leaf a cosmic tale,
In whispered winds that gently sail.

The heavens arch in hues divine,
With constellations woven fine.
In the embrace of ancient woods,
The quiet magic lifts our moods.

The gentle hum of nature's heart,
A symphony, a work of art.
The wilderness wears the sky's bright score,
A celestial weave forevermore.

So walk beneath this vast expanse,
Let starlit wonders stir your chance.
In every step, let freedom rise,
Awake your spirit to the skies.

Secrets of the Rooted Elders

Beneath the surface, secrets lie,
In whispered roots that intertwine.
The ancient tales of ages past,
In earthy depths, their shadows cast.

The wisdom held in bark and leaf,
A legacy of joy and grief.
In gnarled branches, stories dwell,
Of every storm, of every spell.

With every cycle of the moon,
The elders sing a timeless tune.
In quietude, they stand their ground,
Their twisted forms both wise and sound.

They anchor dreams, they hold the sky,
In roots of strength, the years comply.
With every season's endless sway,
The truths of life find their way.

So listen close, for they will share,
The whispers of the earth, laid bare.
In every shadow, every shade,
The secrets of the rooted stay.

Reflections in the Twisted Trellis

In gardens wild, the trellises twist,
A tangled maze of light and mist.
Each leaf a mirror, every vine,
Reflecting dreams in soft design.

The colors dance in dappled grace,
With blossoms bright, a warm embrace.
And in the twilight, shadows blend,
A gentle heart, a friend, a friend.

Through arches bent in nature's hand,
The echoes of the past withstand.
With every bloom, a story's spun,
Where laughter blooms beneath the sun.

Oh, twisted trellis, harbor light,
In depths of dark, a glimpse of bright.
Each turning path, a route to find,
The hidden wonders intertwined.

So let your heart take wing and float,
In reflections where the soul can gloat.
In every corner, every turn,
The trellis waits, and hearts will yearn.

Enigmas of Green Amongst the Peaks

In shadows deep where secrets lie,
Emerald whispers dance on high.
Mossy stones and ancient trees,
Guard the tales of Earth's decrees.

Mountains sigh with stories untold,
Wrapped in veils of misty gold.
Each breeze a riddle, soft yet clear,
Echoing magic that draws us near.

Branches weaving a timeless thread,
Where dreams awaken, fears are shed.
A kingdom where the wild winds roam,
In every crevice, call it home.

Footfalls trace the paths of lore,
Searching for what lies in store.
Mysterious blooms in the dappled light,
Enchant the heart through day and night.

Amongst the peaks, an age-old quest,
Reveals the soul, ignites the rest.
In nature's arms, we find our part,
As enigmas cradle every heart.

Luminescent Threads of Nature's Cloak

Beneath the barrow of twilight's gleam,
Threads of silver weave a dream.
Stars like lanterns pierce the night,
Guiding lost souls with their light.

Flickers dance on the forest floor,
Illuminating tales of yore.
Ferns unfurl like whispers bright,
Adorning shadows with pure delight.

In every droplet, rainbows bloom,
As nature's brush sweeps up the gloom.
Each petal glows, a canvas rare,
Crafting beauty from the air.

Crickets play their serenade,
Beneath the boughs where dreams are made.
Night unfolds with a gentle sigh,
As luminescent wonders fly.

Nature dons her cloaks of grace,
In every corner, every space.
With threads of gold and shades of blue,
The magic lingers, ever true.

Rhythms in the Petals' Embrace

In gardens where the roses sway,
Petals whisper what words convey.
Each hue a story, soft and sweet,
In nature's rhythm, hearts do meet.

The bees hum tunes with busy flight,
As blooms awaken to morning light.
Their fragrant laughter fills the air,
In every moment, magic rare.

Tulips bow with spring's soft breath,
Dancing lightly, defying death.
In every bud, a promise grows,
Of beauty hidden, life bestows.

Daisies sway in the summer sun,
In playful circles, joy has spun.
Their petals form a gentle rhyme,
Reminding us to cherish time.

As autumn paints in gold and red,
With every leaf, a story spread.
The rhythms sway, the garden hums,
In petals' embrace, true peace comes.

Journey Beneath the Whispering Thickets

Beneath the thickets, secrets hide,
In whispering leaves, the spirits glide.
A path unfolds, mysterious, wide,
Where echoes of the past abide.

In twilight's glow, we wander slow,
With every step, the shadows grow.
Bramble and bracken guard the way,
As ancient tales weave night and day.

Ferns unfurl with a gentle sigh,
Inviting the stars to light the sky.
Each rustle tells of those who've tread,
The stories linger, love and dread.

Time slips softly, like a stream,
Carrying whispers, weaving dreams.
The heartbeats echo through every pine,
In this enchanted realm, divine.

A journey taken, hand in hand,
Beneath this thicket, we understand.
In nature's arms, together we find,
The magic of the heart and mind.

Essence of the Verdant Labyrinth

In shadows deep where secrets lie,
The emerald leaves begin to sigh.
Whispers dance on a gentle breeze,
Entwined with tales of ancient trees.

A pathway winds through tangled roots,
As sunlight beams in dappled boots.
Creatures peek from mossy homes,
In a world where magic roams.

Petals bloom in radiant hues,
Each color cradles morning's muse.
The air is thick with stories spun,
Of every life beneath the sun.

Cascading waters hum a tune,
Reflecting light of a silver moon.
Each ripple holds a curious spark,
As shadows dance within the dark.

In this labyrinth, dreams unfurl,
A spellbound dance, a mystic swirl.
The heart will find its truest guide,
Where whispers of the woods abide.

Breaths of Life in the Wild Expanse

Across the fields where shadows play,
Nature's breath ignites the day.
In rustling grass, the wild things stir,
Each heartbeat sings, a vibrant purr.

The sun spills gold on verdant blades,
In every corner, joy cascades.
A chorus rings from feathered throats,
As dreams take flight on wind-blown notes.

Upon the hills where freedom flies,
The sky is painted with amber sighs.
With every gust, the spirit soars,
Embracing life, it ever explores.

In every stream, reflections gleam,
Mirroring tales of endless dreams.
The dance of leaves, a woven song,
In wild expanse, where hearts belong.

So let us roam where hope is found,
In open lands, where love is crowned.
With every breath, we taste the light,
In the wild expanse, our souls take flight.

Spheres of Light in Nebulous Ferns

Where shadows blend with whispering light,
In nebulous ferns, a gentle sight.
Each tendril holds a flickering dream,
In the hush of dusk, life's quiet theme.

Luminescent orbs softly glow,
As secrets of the night start to flow.
In twilight's embrace, the magic sings,
Of fairies, wands, and wondrous things.

Through tangled fronds, the stars align,
A dance of fate, a cosmic sign.
In mysteries deep, the heart may find,
A truth untold, a love entwined.

Within the sphere where shadows bend,
The very fabric of dreams transcend.
With every flicker, a story begins,
In nebulous ferns, where light spins.

So wander here where wonders weave,
In ferns that whisper, and hearts believe.
With each soft glow, the world expands,
In spheres of light, where magic stands.

A Tangle of Dreams and Realities

In the web of night where dreams collide,
A tangle forms, a heart's confide.
Threads of hope and strands of fear,
In every whisper, all is clear.

Reality sways, a fragile frame,
As dreams ignite, a wild flame.
In twilight's grasp, they twist and churn,
Each flicker holds a lesson learned.

Daring paths where shadows merge,
The heart's desire begins to surge.
In every corner, visions pulse,
A realm of wonder, an endless impulse.

With every heartbeat, slowly spun,
The tapestry of life is begun.
Weaving threads both dark and bright,
In this dance of day and night.

So come, embrace the tangled way,
Where dreams abound, and fears decay.
In the echo, let your spirit fly,
In a tangle where the soul can sigh.

Palette of Leaves Beneath the Moon

In whispers soft, the branches sway,
The silver light begins to play.
A tapestry of green and gold,
Beneath the moon, their secrets unfold.

With every breeze, a story's spun,
Of elfin realms where dreams have run.
The rustling leaves, they softly croon,
A lullaby beneath the moon.

Emerald hues kissed by the night,
In shimmering shadows, they take flight.
With every glimmering star above,
The leaves dance gently, a tale of love.

A palette bright, a painter's hand,
Brushes the earth, a wild expanse.
In every crinkle, a vibrant tune,
A world awash with silvered bloom.

So linger here, in quiet grace,
Where nature's heart finds its own place.
In palette rich, so bright and bold,
The leaves beneath the moon unfold.

The Sanctuary of Interwoven Shadows

In twilight's breath, the shadows weave,
A haven where the ancients grieve.
Interlaced within the trees,
A sanctuary held in gentle breeze.

Beneath the boughs, tales intertwine,
Of whispered fears and love divine.
With every rustle, a secret told,
Of dreams that shimmer, soft and bold.

The air, a canvas thick with sighs,
Where hidden wonders softly rise.
In tangled limbs, where darkness fights,
A dance of flickering firelight.

A sacred place where spirits roam,
Each leaf and shadow feels like home.
In tangled roots, histories flow,
The sanctuary where shadows glow.

So tread with care, enchanted friend,
In this haven, where journeys blend.
Embrace the dusk, let worries go,
In the sanctuary of shadows, we grow.

Sagas of the Gnarled Keepers

The gnarled trees, like sentinels, stand,
Guardians of secrets, ancient and grand.
Their twisted limbs hold whispered lore,
Of timeworn tales and battles once wore.

With every knot, a story sown,
Of love and loss, deep roots have grown.
In their embrace, the earth does sigh,
As memories echo, never to die.

They watch the stars from their lofty heights,
And cradle dreams in the quiet nights.
The sagas told by leaves that flutter,
In every breeze, a forgotten utter.

Where nature's pulse meets the heart's desire,
In gnarled fingers, the world they inspire.
Through tempest winds and serene calms,
The keepers whisper, their wisdom charms.

Among the roots, the stories spill,
In shadows deep, their echoes thrill.
The gnarled keepers, wise and true,
Hold sagas rich, awaiting you.

Breath of the Nocturnal Foliage

In velvet dusk, the foliage breathes,
With whispered tales that night bequeathes.
Each leaf a flicker, each branch a sigh,
In shadows deep where mysteries lie.

The nightingale sings a haunting song,
Of love that stirs when the dark feels long.
With shimmering notes that twirl and glide,
The breath of foliage becomes our guide.

With gentle grace, the moonlight streams,
Through branches woven with silver dreams.
In every rustle, the world is spun,
A tapestry of the night begun.

Embrace the hush of the starry gloom,
Where every shadow finds its room.
In nocturnal whispers, secrets blend,
The breath of foliage, a timeless friend.

So take a moment, heed the call,
As nature's breath enchants us all.
In every rustle, a heart's delight,
The nocturnal foliage, bathed in light.

Lullabies of the Ivy-Laden Hills

In the twilight's gentle grace,
Whispers of dreams softly trace.
Echoes weave through the trees,
Sending hearts upon the breeze.

Moonlit paths where shadows play,
Guide the lost till break of day.
Stars above like diamonds gleam,
Cradling secrets in their dream.

Ivy vines in emerald wraps,
Guarding stories, hidden maps.
Hush now, listen to the song,
Nature's lullaby flows strong.

Down the hills where fairies dance,
In the glimmers of moon's glance.
Sleepy owls in quiet flight,
Keep the vigil of the night.

Dreamers rest in soft embrace,
In this peaceful, sacred space.
Lullabies from hills afar,
Cradle wishes like a star.

Tales from the Enchanted Green

In the heart of emerald glade,
Magic sparks beneath the shade.
Mossy stones tell tales of yore,
Where whispers echo evermore.

Windswept sighs through branches weave,
Stories told for those who believe.
Squirrels dance and shadows flit,
In this world where time must sit.

Little spirits twirl and sing,
Making every heart take wing.
Beneath the boughs, dreams take flight,
Wrapped in wonder, pure delight.

As sunlight kisses leaves of gold,
Ancient secrets, softly told.
Deer leap softly through the dew,
In the green, so sweet and true.

Listen close; the forest calls,
Magic pulses 'neath its thralls.
Tales of joy, and tales of woe,
In the enchanted green they flow.

Undercurrents of the Verdant Slopes

Through the valleys, whispers sigh,
Glimmering tales that float on high.
Beneath the canopy so wide,
Mysteries in shadows hide.

Rippling streams that gently glide,
Carry secrets, nature's pride.
Pebbles dance in sunlit rays,
Telling stories of the days.

Ferns unfurl like ancient scrolls,
Revealing truths of restless souls.
Every leaf, a chapter spun,
In the land where all is one.

Mountain echoes call to me,
In their depths, I feel so free.
Nature's language, soft and pure,
In these hills, my heart's allure.

Undercurrents, swift and bright,
Guide the lost through darkest night.
In the verdant slopes we roam,
Finding peace, our spirit's home.

Luminous Secrets of Arbor Vistas

In the glen where shadows play,
Luminous secrets light the way.
Beneath the boughs where time is kind,
Magic blooms within the mind.

Glimmers dance on twilight's breath,
Life's sweet nectar, light, and death.
Whispers echo through the leaves,
In this realm, the heart believes.

Every root and branch holds goals,
Tales entwined within their souls.
Night unfolds like velvet skies,
As the cosmos softly sighs.

Winding paths of silver glow,
Willow's tears and twilight's flow.
Watch as constellations weave,
In the night, we dare to dream.

Here, where every moment glows,
Knowledge sprouts like verdant bloes.
Arbor vistas, vast and grand,
Luminous dreams at our command.

Green Fingers on a Gnarled Summit

Amidst the peaks where shadows play,
The green fingers stretch, reaching for day.
In whispers soft, the winds convey,
The secrets held in nature's way.

Gnarled roots dance in the rich, dark soil,
With tender care, the heart to toil.
Each leaf unfurls, a story loyal,
Upon the summit, where dreams uncoil.

Sunrise bathes the world in gold,
While every petal glimmers bold.
On ancient stones, old tales are told,
In every breeze, the magic rolled.

Here blossoms bloom, yet time stands still,
As nature weaves her wondrous thrill.
Through vibrant hues and fragrant will,
The mountain breathes, a realm to fill.

With every step, a spark of cheer,
Nature's laughter ringing clear.
Upon the summit, free from fear,
The heart finds home, forever near.

Secrets Beneath the Twisted Boughs

In tangled woods where shadows creep,
Beneath the boughs, the secrets seep.
In whispered tales, the ancients weep,
As dreams tangled in roots, we keep.

A fae light flickers, softly glows,
In hidden clearings, where magic flows.
The gentle breeze in silence knows,
What the heart wishes, the heart bestows.

Rustling leaves weave ancient lore,
Of wanderers lost and dreams they bore.
Through twisted paths, we seek for more,
In nature's arms, our spirits soar.

With every step upon the path,
The echoes stir, their gentle wrath.
Amongst the trees, we glimpse the math,
Of life entwined in nature's swath.

So venture forth into the night,
Where shadows dance in soft moonlight.
Embrace the wild, the pure delight,
For beneath twisted boughs, there's flight.

The Serpent's Embrace of Twists

In twisting paths where shadows coil,
The serpent's dance with silent toil.
Through emerald hues, a secret soil,
Embracing life in nature's spoil.

Around the roots, the whispers sigh,
Inviting all to linger nigh.
With emerald grace, the serpent sly,
Beneath the boughs, where dreams can fly.

Each turn reveals a haunting glance,
Where echoes weave a timeless dance.
In stillness found, we take our chance,
In nature's arms, our hearts shall prance.

The sky above is painted blue,
As stories old in whispers grew.
Amongst the leaves, a world anew,
Awaits the brave, the heart so true.

Through winding trails, lost, yet free,
The serpent winds its mystery.
And in those twists, we come to see,
The beauty held in nature's glee.

Melody of Leaves in the Breeze

In rustling leaves, a melody plays,
A symphony bright through sunlit rays.
With every wind, the forest sways,
In harmony found, the heart obeys.

As branches sway with playful grace,
The whispers blend in nature's space.
Each note a story, each turn a trace,
Of lives once lived, in this embrace.

Through dancing ferns, the music flows,
Creating dreams where wonder grows.
In every breeze, the spirit knows,
The gentle hand of time that shows.

At dusk, when shadows softly creep,
The melody calls from woods so deep.
In twilight still, our hearts shall leap,
As nature cradles us in sleep.

So close your eyes and hear the sound,
The leaves performing all around.
In every whisper, love is found,
A melody of life, profound.

The Veil of Time in the Green Halls

In the green halls where whispers dwell,
Time drapes its secrets, a woven spell.
Moonlight dances on emerald leaves,
While shadows weave tales that never leave.

Ancient roots twist under the ground,
Echoes of laughter and dreams abound.
Footsteps forgotten in soft, rich loam,
The heart finds peace in this timeless home.

Glimmers of sunlight break through the shade,
Illuminating paths where magic's made.
Each breath a promise, each sigh a song,
In this sacred place where spirits belong.

The veil of history hangs thick in the air,
Silhouettes flicker—ghosts linger there.
Underneath whispers, a pulse, a beat,
In harmony found, with eternity meet.

So linger a while, let wonder ignite,
In the green halls, bathed in soft light.
For time is a tapestry, ever unfurled,
Woven from magic, within this world.

Murmurs of Life in Nature's Nest

In the cradle of leaves, where the soft winds sigh,
Nature hums gently, a lullaby.
Buds unfurl as dawn starts to creep,
In the heart of the woods, life stirs from sleep.

Whispers of brooklets, a babbling rhyme,
Carry tales of the earth, intertwined with time.
Above, a lark sings, pure and so sweet,
Each note dances lightly on dew-drenched feet.

Under the boughs, where shadows play,
The wildflowers bloom with colors of May.
Sunbeams cascade through branches like lace,
In this tranquil haven, find your place.

From rustling grasses to chirping bees,
Every sound is a song carried on the breeze.
In this tender refuge, nature's embrace,
Feel the pulse of the earth, a divine grace.

Murmurs of life thrive in every nook,
In quiet corners, the world's storybook.
So lean in close and listen well,
For in nature's nest, there's magic to tell.

Silken Shadows of the Verdant Realm

In the verdant realm where shadows weave,
Dreams take flight, and spirits believe.
Silken threads of twilight spin,
Whispers of magic invite you in.

Beneath the canopy, secrets unwind,
Lost in the patterns that nature designed.
Glades, like mirrors, reflect the sky,
Holding the dreams of those who pass by.

Creeping tendrils in twilight's embrace,
Form intricate paths through this hidden place.
Winds carry laughter, a gentle sigh,
Like echoes of stories that dare to fly.

With every soft step, the shadows gleam,
Awash in glimmers, they stir up a dream.
The air thick with whispers of magic and lore,
In this silent realm, forever explore.

A dance of the wild, a tapestry spun,
Under moonlight's watch, each story begun.
In silken shadows, let your heart roam,
For in the verdant realm, you find your home.

Labyrinthine Paths in the Forest's Heart

In the forest's heart, where secrets blend,
Labyrinthine paths twist and extend.
Each turn reveals a tale to be told,
Of ancient trees and whispers of old.

Beneath the ferns, where the wild things grow,
Mysteries linger in the soft, low glow.
Footfalls softly muted by mossy delight,
In this woven wonder, both eerie and bright.

Sunlight filters through branches entwined,
Crafting patterns that dance, undefined.
The call of the wild sings deep in your soul,
In this magical maze, you become whole.

Winding through shadows, a journey profound,
Every corner turned, new wonders are found.
With each whispered breeze and rustling leaf,
Your heart finds solace, in joy and belief.

In the forest's heart, where paths intertwine,
You'll lose yourself gently in nature's design.
So wander with wonder, let your spirit take flight,
For in this labyrinth, all feels just right.

The Ivy's Dance under the Moonlight

In silver beams, the ivy twirls,
A dance of shadows, whispered swirls.
Beneath the moon's soft, watchful glow,
She weaves her tale, both sweet and slow.

The nightingale sings through the air,
While twinkling stars weave dreams to share.
Each tender leaf, a secret told,
In shimmering light, their stories unfold.

With every sway, a magic unfolds,
Of ancient tales, of knights and gold.
The ivy knows where dreams do tread,
In the heart of woods, where all is said.

As night descends, the world is still,
In moonlit silence, dreams can fill.
The ivy dances, free and wild,
A graceful spirit, nature's child.

In twilight's arms, she finds her grace,
A hidden world, a sacred space.
So let us linger, hearts awake,
And join the ivy's dance, for love's sake.

Nature's Embrace in Forgotten Places

In shadowed groves, where whispers lie,
Nature's embrace holds secrets shy.
Wildflower blooms in softest hues,
While ancient oaks share timeless views.

A brook winds softly, a lullaby,
Its gentle song flows, a soothing sigh.
Among the stones where mosses creep,
In soft retreat, the heart finds peace.

When twilight falls, a magic stirs,
As fireflies dance in gentle spur.
The night reveals a hidden grace,
In forgotten places, time finds space.

An echo of laughter fills the air,
A melody born from tender care.
Each breath of wind a lover's sigh,
In nature's arms, our spirits fly.

So wanders here, find solace true,
In every shade of deepest blue.
Embrace the stillness, let love grow,
In forgotten places, let hearts flow.

Tales from the Amethyst Canopy

Beneath the boughs of amethyst hue,
The forest holds tales, old yet true.
A whispering breeze, a fluttering leaf,
Each story laced with joy and grief.

The owls, they hoot, a wise refrain,
Guardians of secrets, of joy and pain.
They see the dance of shadows play,
Where legends breathe, and dreams sway.

In twilight's grip, the colors blend,
The sun bows low, the daylight ends.
And with the stars, the stories rise,
In every glimmer, a world lies.

From lilac blooms to emerald ferns,
The canopy sways, and each heart yearns.
For tales of magic, love's embrace,
In nature's realm, a sacred space.

So tread with care beneath this dome,
For every step, you're never alone.
In the amethyst canopy, tales are spun,
A bond with nature, forever begun.

Treasures Hidden in the Cascading Leaves

In forests deep where shadows play,
Treasures bloom in soft array.
Cascading leaves hide glimmers bright,
Secrets waiting for the light.

A patter of rain, a lover's dance,
In nature's heart, the world's expanse.
Each leaf a jewel, a story spun,
Whispers of earth, of moon, of sun.

Beneath the boughs, a symphony,
Of rustling leaves, a melody.
With every rustle, dreams unfold,
In treasures hidden, life untold.

The breeze carries laughter, soft and sweet,
A gentle reminder of love's heartbeat.
The treasures wait for those who seek,
In cascading leaves, their secrets speak.

So wander forth where nature breathes,
In every path, the heart believes.
For hidden treasures in the trees,
Are whispers of life in the gentle breeze.

Threads in a Mythic Tangle

In shadowed realms where secrets dwell,
The whispers weave a timeless spell.
A tapestry of fate is spun,
Each thread a tale, each tale begun.

With every knot, a story grows,
In the tangled mess, magic glows.
Ancient hearts in silence bind,
The lore of ages intertwined.

Beneath the stars, the weavers sigh,
As dreams take flight, in night's dark sky.
A flicker of hope, a spark of light,
In mythic tangle, shadows fight.

Threads of laughter, threads of tears,
Interwoven through the years.
In every twist, a fate entwined,
A thread unbroken, so aligned.

Through time and space, their stories dance,
In every heart, a fleeting glance.
Yet in this weave, we shall find,
The strength of souls forever entwined.

Echoes of the Forest's Heart

In twilight's glow, the forest sighs,
With whispers soft that bring forth ties.
Each leaf a story, each branch a tale,
In the heart of wood, dreams set sail.

The rustle speaks of ages past,
Of lively spirits, shadows cast.
With every step, the echoes play,
As nature's voice guides our way.

Moonbeams filter through the green,
An ancient dance, forever seen.
In every sound, a melody,
The forest sings, wild and free.

Beneath the boughs where magic streams,
Life weaves through vibrant dreams.
A cradle of whispers, soft and pure,
In the forest's heart, we endure.

History breathes in each gentle sway,
As night unfolds into a new day.
Across the branches, shadows blend,
In echoes deep, our spirits mend.

The Dance of Light Through Foliage

In dappled shades where sunbeams play,
The leaves twist gently, night and day.
A ballet spun on wind's soft breath,
Through emerald thickets, life and death.

Light twirls around each fragile stem,
A fleeting glance, a luminous gem.
Illumination flickers bright,
In nature's stage, the dance of light.

As hours pass, the shadows creep,
Through golden beams, where secrets seep.
In this waltz of shade and warmth,
We find our place, our truest forms.

Every flicker, a promise made,
In this light, dreams never fade.
A timeless rhythm, a sacred trust,
In the heart of foliage, as we must.

Through rustling leaves, the stories soar,
In golden glitter, forevermore.
The dance of light, in endless flight,
Guides our hearts through day and night.

Woven Dreams of Earth and Sky

In twilight's grasp, the dreams take flight,
Where earth meets sky in hues of light.
From whispered wishes, the stars ignite,
A cosmic dance, both bold and bright.

With every breath, the world unfolds,
In stories spun, the heart beholds.
Dreams of soil, and skies so vast,
In woven patterns, futures cast.

The mountains high, the rivers wide,
In nature's embrace, our hopes abide.
With every dawn, a chance anew,
As earth and sky paint worlds in blue.

Threads of starlight, roots in the ground,
In harmony, our spirits found.
A gentle pull, the heartstrings play,
In dreams woven, they guide our way.

Through cosmic dance and earthly grace,
In every heartbeat, we find our place.
Woven dreams shall ever sigh,
In union, earth and limitless sky.

The Grasp of Nature's Breath

In whispers soft, the wind calls near,
Among the trees where silence sears.
Leaves flutter gently, tales they weave,
With every sigh, the world believes.

The brook sings sweet, a melodic drift,
Guiding wanderers, through nature's gift.
Each step echoes on earthen paths,
Marking journeys, igniting laughs.

Moonlit nights, where shadows creep,
Crickets serenade dreams to sleep.
Stars above, like diamonds glow,
In the embrace of night, we grow.

A tapestry of colors bright,
Nature's brush strokes, pure delight.
Breezes stoke the flames of fire,
In this realm, hearts never tire.

With every breath, the earth unfolds,
Secrets hidden, stories told.
In nature's clasp, we find our place,
A tender, everlasting grace.

Chronicle of Quiet Wanderings

Upon the hills where whispers dwell,
A tale unfolds, as stones compel.
Step by step, the path unwinds,
In every nook, a thought it finds.

Moss blankets rocks in cradled rest,
The heart beats soft, embraced, blessed.
With every twist, a secret peeks,
In twilight's hush, the silence speaks.

Gentle streams weave tales of old,
Reflecting dreams that hearts once told.
Footprints trail like fleeting stars,
Guided gently by nature's scars.

The sun dips low, casting golden rays,
Painting memories in magical ways.
In rustling leaves, adventures sway,
Echoing softly, where wanderers play.

As night descends, the world slows down,
Beneath the cloak of a twilight crown.
Each moment lingers, whispers abide,
In the quiet glow of the evening tide.

Glistening Hues of Forgotten Trails

Emerald greens on paths of gold,
Each step we take, a story bold.
Nature's palette sings and sways,
In hues of old, where magic lays.

Twilight carpets the forest floor,
Leading us onward, forever more.
With each soft rustle of the leaves,
A gentle dance, the heart believes.

Murmur of streams in secret glades,
Whispered dreams in sylvan shades.
Wildflowers bloom, in splendor bright,
Painting the dusk with pure delight.

Clouds unfurl, painting skies ajar,
Chasing horizons, where wonders are.
In every shadow, tales arise,
Of lost treasures and far-off skies.

Embrace the scent of earth and rain,
In nature's heart, we break the chain.
Glistening hues that guide the way,
In forgotten trails, forever stay.

The Arboreal Legacy Unfurled

In tangled roots, the whispers twine,
Ancient trees with stories fine.
Branches cradle the dreams of old,
In every ring, a tale retold.

Leaves flutter down like fleeting days,
Golden memories, in sunlit rays.
Every bough bears witness clear,
To joy and sorrow, love and fear.

A symphony sung by rustling green,
In lightly danced shadows, we glean.
Seasons change, yet they remain,
Guardians true of beauty and pain.

Bark weathers storms, yet bends with grace,
Life's ebb and flow in this sacred space.
Roots dig deep in soft, warm earth,
From such strength springs endless worth.

In this legacy, we find our part,
With every whisper, they touch the heart.
The arboreal realm, forever bright,
Guiding our souls with its ancient light.

Sanctum of the Shaded Glade

In whispers soft, the shadows dwell,
Where ancient trees weave time's own spell.
A hidden path where dreams reside,
In every leaf, a secret confide.

The brook hums tunes of ages past,
In mossy realms, the die is cast.
With laughter low, the pixies play,
Their magic blooms in the emerald sway.

The sun dips low, the night unfolds,
In twilight's grip, the story molds.
A tapestry of stars awakes,
In silver beams, the glade partakes.

With every breath, the forest sighs,
As twilight paints the indigo skies.
In this sanctum, peace prevails,
As time drifts softly, wrapped in veils.

Nature's Notes in the Early Dawn

As dawn's first light breaks through the mist,
The world awakens, not one soul missed.
A symphony of chirps and calls,
In every creature, the music enthralls.

The gentle breeze does play its tune,
Dancing 'neath the sleepy moon.
In blossoms bright, the colors gleam,
Nature's notes weave the morning dream.

Beneath the trees, the shadows fade,
Awakening life in the soft glade.
Each fluttered wing, each rustled leaf,
Brings whispers sweet of joy and grief.

The sun ascends with golden grace,
Lighting hearts and every place.
In creatures small and mighty skies,
Nature's breath, a soft reprise.

Each droplet shines like polished glass,
In dewy wonder, moments pass.
With every heartbeat, hope renews,
As day unfolds with vibrant hues.

Seeds of Reverie in Twilight's Hold

In twilight's hush, the dreams take flight,
As shadows blend in the soft twilight.
Each whisper carries a wish untold,
In secret corners where hearts unfold.

The stars emerge with a gentle glow,
As memories rush like a winding flow.
In every heartbeat, stories weave,
Of laughter, love, and what we believe.

The garden blooms with whispers sweet,
In every petal, life's heartbeat.
The breeze caresses and softly stirs,
In every rustle, magic occurs.

Gather the seeds in the dusk's embrace,
Hopes planted deep in this sacred space.
Quiet moments, where dreams may thrive,
In twilight's hold, we come alive.

With every shadow, a path appears,
Guiding our thoughts through hopes and fears.
As starlight dances on velvet skies,
The seeds of reverie begin to rise.

Arcane Roots in the Faerie Grove

In a grove where whispers weave the night,
The faeries dance in the soft moonlight.
With arcane roots that grip the ground,
In twinkling air, magic is found.

Beneath the boughs, the old ones speak,
In ancient tongues, secrets they seek.
In emerald shadows, stories unfold,
Of twilight tales and dawns of gold.

The glimmering mist holds stories near,
Of every wish and whispered fear.
With laughter sweet, the faeries roam,
In every heart, they find a home.

In the moonlit glow, dreams take flight,
With every twirl, they chase the night.
In sacred spaces, wonder breeds,
In the faerie grove, with arcane seeds.

As morning's light begins to creep,
The faeries gather, the world to keep.
In every leaf, in every stone,
The magic lingers, never alone.

The Cloak of Wonder Draped in Green

Beneath the boughs, the whispers flow,
In emerald hues, where secrets glow.
A cloak of wonder, softly spun,
Enfolds the earth, with magic run.

With every leaf, a tale is told,
Of ancient spirits, brave and bold.
Through dappled light, the shadows dance,
Inviting hearts to take a chance.

The streams will sing, the wind will sigh,
As dreams awaken, soaring high.
In hidden glades, the paths entwine,
In nature's heart, we seek the divine.

Oh, how the flowers fiercely bloom,
In vibrant hues, dispelling gloom.
The cloak of green, it wraps us tight,
An ever-present, guiding light.

So wander deep where wonders call,
Let magic lead, let spirits sprawl.
In every step, the world will gleam,
Awake within this timeless dream.

Tapestry of Life Between the Stones

Amidst the stones, the stories weave,
A tapestry of hopes, believe.
Through cracks and crevices, life defies,
While nature paints the endless skies.

Each pebble tells of years gone by,
With timeless echoes, soft and shy.
The roots reach deep, in search of spark,
A vibrant dance within the dark.

The lichen blooms, a subtle grace,
In harmony, they find their place.
With sunlit threads, the days unfold,
A rich design, both brave and bold.

The whispered winds shall carry on,
The songs of life, from dusk to dawn.
Each stitch in time, a memory,
A bond unbroken, endlessly.

So linger where the moments flow,
Between the stones, let magic grow.
In every layer, love does remain,
A tapestry of joy and pain.

Fables Woven in Tendril and Thorn

In every tendril, tales are spun,
Beneath the thorns, the fears are won.
A whispering breeze, it carries lore,
Of battles fought and hearts that soar.

The shadows linger, secrets keep,
As wildflowers in silence creep.
With each embrace, the vines entwine,
Creating bonds that rarely shine.

With every thorn, a lesson learned,
In pain, the strength of trust is earned.
Through tangled roots, the courage grows,
In fables shared, the wisdom flows.

So pause beneath the ancient trees,
And listen close to every breeze.
In nature's arms, the world's unspun,
Fables woven, never done.

The heart will yearn, the soul will ache,
For stories etched in every break.
Within the dark, a light is sworn,
A fable sung in tendril and thorn.

Shadows Dancing on the Ancient Rocks

On ancient rocks, where shadows play,
A dance of time, both night and day.
With every step, the echoes sigh,
As whispers of the past drift by.

Beneath the moon, the stories glow,
Of endless skies and winds that blow.
With every flicker, dreams untold,
As mysteries of ages unfold.

The stones remember all that's been,
In silent witness, truths are seen.
With every shadow cast, we find,
The depths of heart, the strength of mind.

So let the night enfold us whole,
As shadows weave and spirits stroll.
Together here, where light reveals,
The sacred bond that time conceals.

In every crevice, hope resides,
Where ancient echoes still abide.
With shadows dancing on the rocks,
We journey forth, our hearts unblocked.

Hues of the Wild Tangle

In the forest deep, where shadows play,
Whispers of magic float like the day.
Tangles of ivy, bright and alive,
Colors of chaos, where spirits thrive.

Moss carpets ground, a soft emerald bed,
Beneath ancient trees, where secrets are spread.
Crimson and gold shimmer, wildflower bloom,
Nature's own brush paints the darkening gloom.

Rivers of silver with laughter they flow,
Secrets entwined where the wild breezes blow.
Cinnamon scents from the bark of a tree,
Nature's own palette, forever set free.

In each rustling leaf, a tale to be spun,
Of wonders found, or battles once won.
Caught in the moment, the wild tangle speaks,
In hues that enchant, it's the magic we seek.

As twilight descends, the colors do fade,
Yet the spirit of wild shall never be swayed.
For deep in the heart where the wild things roam,
Hues of the tangle, forever our home.

Moonlit Pathways in Verdant Rock

Beneath a moon's smile, the shadows unfurl,
Pathways of silver where dreams gently swirl.
Whispers of night breeze through branches so fair,
A lantern of stars in the cool evening air.

Verdant the rocks where the soft moss has grown,
Secrets of ages in whispers are sewn.
Crickets sing softly, a sweet lullaby,
Under the gaze of the vast, glinting sky.

Each step is a dance on the edges of light,
A journey of wonder, of beauty in flight.
Curves of the pathway like ribbons they weave,
Drawing us deeper till hearts dare believe.

Twilight embraces the world in its charms,
Nature unfolds, and we fall into arms.
With each passing moment, the night starts to glow,
In moonlit pathways, our spirits shall flow.

So join the soft night, where the wild whispers call,
In verdant rock's heart, we shall never fall.
For journeys transcend as the stars lead the way,
In moonlit pathways, forever we'll stay.

Tapestry of Nature's Vein

In the heart of the forest, life's stories are spun,
Threads of vibrant colors, each second a fun.
Woven together in delicate strands,
Nature's own magic crafted by hands.

Cascading waters weave silver and blue,
Dancing and rushing, a joyous debut.
Petals unfold like secrets untold,
Whispers of history in colors of gold.

Every turn of the path, a story to share,
Boughs gently cradle the songs in the air.
Fern leaves a blanket of intricate lace,
Nature's own fabric holds beauty and grace.

As sunsets ignite the horizon's embrace,
Shadows intertwine, leaving only their trace.
A tapestry glimmers with long-lost refrain,
In the veins of the earth, we find love's domain.

With each gentle breeze, the tapestry sways,
Carrying wishes on gossamer rays.
In this vibrant weave, we together remain,
Lost in the beauty, our hearts entertain.

Emblems of the Emerald Realm

In the emerald realm where enchantments abound,
Every leaf sways to the soft, soothing sound.
Ferns jewels of green drape the mossy knoll,
Whispers of magic adorning each soul.

Barriers broken where dreams come alive,
Creatures of whimsy in shadows they thrive.
With echoes of laughter, they dance through the air,
Emblems of wonder, hidden treasures laid bare.

Sunlight like honey drips down through the leaves,
Kissed by the morning, the forest believes.
Fables are carried by winds from the past,
In this emerald world, love's essence is cast.

Beneath the wide sky, the branches embrace,
Nature holds close every intricate trace.
Footsteps are painted on pathways of dreams,
In this realm of emerald, nothing's as it seems.

Where whispers of magic forever unwind,
Each step in the wild grants the heart peace of mind.
So journey through this realm where we find our theme,
In the emblems of nature, we weave our dream.

Seraphim's Journey in the Grove

In the hush of golden leaves,
A seraph glides with gentle ease,
Each footfall whispers secrets old,
Among the trees, the stories unfold.

A shimmering light with wings so wide,
Guides lost souls where dreams abide,
Through dappled paths of emerald hues,
In the heart of the woods, magic ensues.

With every step, the shadows dance,
In the twilight, they take their chance,
To twirl and spin, in soft twilight,
Embraced by stars, a celestial sight.

Echoes of laughter drift through air,
Unseen hands weave a tapestry rare,
Of friendship forged in moments dear,
Once known to the heart, now crystal clear.

The journey flows like tranquil streams,
Through realms of wonder and whispered dreams,
As seraphs weave their destinies tight,
Together, they soar into the night.

Mysteries Shrouded in Ivy

In shadows deep, where ivy twines,
Lies a world spun with ancient signs,
Whispers of time in every fold,
Stories hidden, waiting to be told.

The moonlit path, a silent guide,
Reveals the secrets ivy can hide,
With tendrils reaching, stories blend,
Nature's embrace, a faithful friend.

Secrets murmur in the dusk,
Of quiet dreams and faded husk,
A dance of silence, stars alight,
Mysteries bloom beneath the night.

Footfalls echo through lush green halls,
Where shadows play and nightingale calls,
Each turn revealing the magic sown,
In the heart of places long overgrown.

Glimmers fade as morning breaks,
Yet in the ivy, still it wakes,
A tapestry of lore and song,
In those dark corners, they still belong.

Whims of Nature on Elevated Ground

Upon the cliffs where breezes play,
Nature's whims in bright array,
Trees lean back in the golden sun,
Each moment crafted, yet so fun.

Clouds drift lazily, tales to share,
Dancing softly in the fragrant air,
Where daisies nod and lilies bow,
Nature winks and takes a vow.

Curled ferns hide in shadows deep,
As crickets sing their songs of sleep,
Where echoes of laughter cling so near,
In the wild heart, devoid of fear.

Birds take flight, a vibrant spree,
Painting the heavens, wild and free,
With every chirp, a story spun,
Of whispered dreams and joyful fun.

On elevated ground, the world expands,
A tapestry stitched by unseen hands,
Each gust of wind, a playful muse,
In nature's grasp, we cannot lose.

Enigmatic Bequests of the Woods

Deep within the wooded embrace,
Lies a treasure, a tranquil space,
Echoes of life and laughter blend,
A testament to the earth's true friend.

With every rustle, stories wake,
In every shadow, memories ache,
Forgotten whispers riding the breeze,
An embrace woven through ancient trees.

A compass made of leaf and bark,
Guiding lost souls through the dark,
Each step leads to a hidden truth,
In the heart of nature's unyielding youth.

With silver moons and twilight's grace,
Every creature finds its place,
Secrets passed through roots so deep,
In the woods where the dreamers sleep.

The bequest of nature, profound and wise,
In every corner, a new surprise,
A sanctuary where spirits play,
Whispers in the woods, forever stay.

Whispers in the Canopy

Beneath the leaves, the secrets sway,
In shadows where the fairies play.
Soft murmurs drift on the breeze,
Tales of magic, lost with ease.

In twilight's glow, the owls take flight,
Guardians of the falling night.
Each rustle tells a story old,
Of daring hearts and dreams of gold.

A rustling sound, a fleeting glance,
In enchanted woods, we dare to dance.
While whispers weave through branches high,
A tapestry against the sky.

Bright stars peek through the velvet dark,
Illuminating a hidden spark.
The canopy, a world unseen,
Where wonder glimmers, fresh and green.

With every breeze, a voice does call,
To wanderers who search for all.
In this realm where secrets lie,
The heart finds wings, begins to fly.

Twilight Tendrils of Time

As daylight fades, the shadows creep,
Through tangled roots, they twist and leap.
Each moment captured, softly spun,
Glimmers of twilight, one by one.

Faint echoes of a distant song,
Where ancient trees have stood so long.
The twilight tendrils, thin and frail,
Wrap 'round the dreams, like a delicate veil.

Each whisper speaks of days gone by,
Of laughter echoing, a sigh.
The night unfolds its velvet cloak,
While hidden magic gently stokes.

In the silence, a heartbeat flows,
Where time slips softly, ebbs and grows.
In twilight's grasp, the past awakes,
With secrets shared, for memory's sake.

So linger here where shadows play,
In twilight's breath, we find our way.
For every moment, though it roams,
In tender twilight, we find our homes.

Shadows of the Ancient Arbor

In the heart of the forest, strong and wide,
Ancient oaks stand, with time as their guide.
Their gnarled branches, a history spun,
Guardians of tales lost, never undone.

Beneath their boughs, soft creatures nest,
In the calm embrace, they find their rest.
The air is thick with secrets spun,
In shadows where daylight comes undone.

A whisper of wind through leaves does glide,
Unraveling mysteries, deep and tied.
In every shadow, a flicker of light,
Holds the echoes of a bygone night.

The roots entwined with the earth's own heart,
A dance of life, where all play their part.
In the ancient arbor, strength prevails,
As time stands still, through haunting tales.

So tread with care in this sacred space,
Where shadows linger, and memories trace.
For here in whispers, the past will roam,
In the ancient's arms, we find our home.

Enchanted Clusters in the Glade

In the glade where dreams take flight,
Enchanted clusters glimmer bright.
Mushrooms glow in softest hue,
As fireflies weave through midnight's dew.

Each petal whispers magic's name,
A world untouched, wild, and untame.
The air is thick with wonder's sighs,
Underneath a tapestry of skies.

In pairs, the blossoms gently sway,
Drawing forth the night's sweet play.
Each fragrant bloom, a promise held,
In secret gardens, love compelled.

Around the bend, where magic clings,
The melody of nature sings.
The glade, a canvas, alive with dreams,
Captured moments in moonlit beams.

So wander here where fairies tread,
In enchanted spaces softly spread.
For in this glade, our hearts are free,
To dance with echoes of what could be.

Ephemeral Beauty on the Rising Mound

Amidst the mist, a blossom sways,
Soft whispers of the dawn's embrace.
Golden rays on petals lay,
A fleeting moment, time's sweet grace.

Each gust of wind, a lover's sigh,
In the stillness, magic weaves.
Beneath the vast and open sky,
Nature dances, heart believes.

The towering mound, a secret tale,
Of laughter lost and dreams untold.
In every droplet, peace prevails,
As wonders in the day unfold.

With every hue, the colors blend,
A fleeting glimpse of life's own art.
The beauty born, as seasons end,
Forever etched within the heart.

Voices of the Wild in Lush Canopies

In emerald woods, where shadows play,
The chorus blooms with every sound.
A symphony of night and day,
In secret realms, enchantment found.

Wisps of light through branches spill,
Soft murmurs of the ancient trees.
Nature's breath, a timeless thrill,
Upon the air, a gentle breeze.

The creatures stir in silent grace,
With tiny feet, they roam and weave.
In hidden nooks, they find their space,
In twilight's glow, they dance and leave.

From rustling leaves, a tale is spun,
Of whispered dreams beneath the sky.
In every leap and hidden run,
The wildest hearts are ever nigh.

The Forgotten Path of Fragrant Blooms

Along the trail where shadows blend,
The blooms of yesteryear reside.
A fragrant tale of time to bend,
In petals soft, the dreams abide.

Each step we take, a gentle kiss,
On natures gift, the past awakes.
In quiet moments, feel the bliss,
Of every path and how it makes.

The overgrown, a tale untold,
Of laughter, whispers, joys and fears.
With scents of lavender and marigold,
The heart remembers what it hears.

Beneath the arch of willow's grace,
In solitude, the spirit climbs.
A dance with time in sacred space,
Embracing yesterday's sweet rhymes.

Harmony Found in the Twine of Time

In the weave of day and night,
The threads of fate begin to sway.
With every heartbeat, life ignites,
A symphony of love's ballet.

Each moment holds a whispered tune,
As stars align in soft embrace.
The monsoon's rain or sun's bright noon,
In nature's grip, we find our place.

With time's embrace, the stories grow,
Connected paths, entwined will be.
Through every ebb and gentle flow,
We dance along life's melody.

In twilight's glow, and dawn's first light,
The harmony of hearts will cling.
Together we shall rise in flight,
In unity, our spirits sing.

Patterns of Growth Under Moon Shadows

In shadows deep, the seedlings sprout,
Their whispers soft, a gentle shout.
Beneath the glow of silver light,
They dance and sway in dreams of night.

The earth, a quilt of velvet green,
With secrets hidden, barely seen.
Each petal opens, revealing grace,
A symphony in nature's embrace.

As tendrils reach for starlit skies,
The blossoms bloom, where magic lies.
In moonlit hours, they twist and turn,
A silent tale, a fire that burns.

The roots entwined, a silent pact,
In harmony, they merge and act.
A tapestry of life unfolds,
In whispers soft, their story told.

Through shadowed paths, their journeys chart,
In every seed, there hides a heart.
With every breath, they learn to grow,
A dance of life beneath the glow.

The Poetry of Tangles and Twists

In tangled roots, the stories spun,
Of ancient lore and battles won.
Each twist and turn, a line of fate,
In woven strands, we navigate.

The brambles weave a mystic thread,
With every path, a word unsaid.
In shadows cast by moon's embrace,
The wild embrace, a sacred space.

With every pull, the whispers sing,
A melody of earth's own spring.
The colors clash, yet find their peace,
In tangled dance, the worries cease.

Beneath the canopy, time slows down,
The silence wears a leafy crown.
In every turn, a secret cost,
In nature's art, we find the lost.

So venture forth, through thickets dense,
In whispers near, the heart's suspense.
Embrace the chaos, find your way,
In tangled paths, let spirit play.

Heartbeats of Nature's Storytellers

In every breeze, the tales unfold,
With rustling leaves, their voices bold.
The heartbeat echoes, soft and clear,
In rhythms ancient, ever near.

The birds, they chirp a symphony,
Composing songs of earth and sea.
Each flutter, each soft rise and fall,
A heartbeat shared, a nature's call.

The rippling streams, they laugh and flow,
With secrets only they can know.
In water's song, a tale is spun,
Of life renewed, of days begun.

The mountains whisper of the years,
A chronicle in stone appears.
Each echo brings a lesson learned,
In nature's heart, our spirits turned.

So pause to hear the world around,
In every breath, a truth is found.
For nature speaks in silent ways,
In heartbeats soft, our spirits graze.

Echoing Vistas Where Magic Dwells

In distant hills, the echoes play,
A haunting tune at end of day.
Where valleys stretch and skies unfold,
The stories whispered, bold and old.

The river charts its winding course,
In magic's grip, a primal force.
With every bend, a world anew,
In reflections deep, the dreams break through.

The stars above, like candles bright,
Illuminate the canvas night.
With dreams alight, they guide the way,
In cosmic dance, the spirits sway.

The winds carry tales of times forgotten,
Through fields of gold, where dreams are sown.
With every gust, a hope ignites,
In echoing vistas, where magic lights.

So wander forth, let wonder guide,
In every step, let love reside.
For in this world of swirling grace,
The whispers dwell, a warm embrace.